Angel
A Walking Miracle

Angela Marie Wood

Angel A Walking Miracle

All Scripture quotations are taken from the King James Version of the Holy Bible (in the public domain.)

ISBN-13: 978-0-9892213-6-8

ISBN-10: 0-9892213-6-9

Printed in the United States of America

RevMedia Publishing
PO BOX 5172
Kingwood, TX 77325

A publishing division of Revelation Ministries

www.revmediapublishing.com

Dedication

To my mom, my best friend: We do everything together. You have sacrificed so much for me. I love you more than I can ever say or show.

To my dad, my partner in the ministry: My teacher, pastor, and example of how to be a Christian father. Thanks, Dad, for typing and preparing the manuscript. You're my favorite preacher.

To my big brother: Thanks for being so strong and supportive of me all these years. I look up to you and I am so proud of what you have accomplished with your life.

To my grandparents Ken (PaPa), and Lois (Nanny) Kennedy who accepted me just the way I was born, but always showed me in a loving, teaching way, that I didn't have to accept the reports I was given and could reach for the stars and attain them. I love you, Nanny and PaPa.

To all the pastors around the United States who have allowed me to stand behind their pulpits and share what God has done in my life. Thanks for believing in me.

Most importantly, I thank God Almighty for His miracle working power that I stand in awe of everyday. Thank you Jesus Christ, because it is through You I can do all things. Thank you Holy Spirit, my friend, for giving me the power to keep on sharing this story.

Foreword

Our precious Angel... From the time she was born she has been our precious Angel. When the doctor laid her in my arms I knew she was special. We have had a lot of hurdles to overcome, but through the grace of God we have come through them all. Angel is an overcomer and she knows and has no doubts that God can help her do anything she needs to do.

Angel, you mean the world to your daddy and me. You have shown us what a walking miracle is. You have so much love and compassion for people and are such a mighty intercessor that it amazes us. When people ask you to pray for them, you don't quit until they have their answer. I thank God that He chose us to be your parents and I know that He has so much more work for you to do. We will just sit back and see what the Lord is going to do in your life because we know it will be exciting. Thank you Lord for our PRECIOUS ANGEL!

Deena & Gary Wood

What an honor to speak about Angel and her book. My wife, Brenda, and I have known Angel since she was twelve years old. Our blessing from Angel is that she adopted us as Uncle Ed and Aunt Brenda. She is one of the few people that "What you see is not what you get." I have watched her grow physically into womanhood and spiritually into an extraordinary witness for our Lord Jesus Christ. In fact, I had the privilege of ordaining Angel into the ministry several years ago, never having to take the thought that she would not or could not uphold the integrity of being a minister of the Gospel. Angel has a special call upon her life of manifesting the fruit of love and joy. She also has put to memory more scripture than anyone I have ever met. As you read this book, share with Angel her life of pressing toward the mark of the high call. Always looking for- ward to new areas of ministry and far exceeding what to some would be too challenging.

Pastor Edgar Lee Adamson
Paris Christian Center
Paris, Tennessee

November 7, 1999

I have known Angela Wood, daughter of Evangelist Gary and Deena Wood, for many years. Angel, as I personally refer to her, is an ordained minister of the Gospel, and has ministered with her parents all over the United States and in foreign countries, sharing her testimony of how God healed her and has given her a ministry in song and the Word of God. Angel is anointed of God to worship and praise the Lord, pray for the sick, and preach the Good News about Jesus Christ. She is a bold witness for Jesus, is focused on winning people to Jesus, and has a pure heart after God. She is a very loving, kind; gentle and forgiving person who lets Jesus love others through her life. Angel is a true handmaiden of the Lord, and a blessing to everyone who knows her.

Sincerely in Christ,
Renee Branson
Director of Mountain Top Ministries
Houston, Texas

The Wood family went to a church I pastored for a number of years. One day Brother Gary was preaching in a service and realized that the building we were meeting in once was a pharmacy. Years ago, when Angel was a very small girl, a very sick little girl, Gary and Deena came here to buy prescriptions for her because she had severe allergies. The stage he was preaching from was once where the pharmacist dispensed the drugs that saved her life. It used to have a sign that read RX prescriptions and now it says JESUS IS LORD. We watched Angel grow from a little girl into a grown woman of God. She is healed by the power of God and all she says comes from the depths of her heart. She is a sweet, anointed woman of God. We appreciate the opportunity to write these words about Angel.

Pastor Steve O"Donohoe
Grace Community Church
Clear Lake City, TX

Angel Marie Wood has been my special friend for many years now, and she is a tremendous blessing to me. She prays for me and often drops me notes to let me know she is praying. I thank God for her, and for the way her life has turned around, simply because her mother and dad would not let her remain the way she was when she was born. The Word of God has brought Angel out of a life of despair and sadness, to a joyous life of blessing and helping others. This book will bless you and help you and inspire you, and especially give courage and hope to those who are fighting some of the same circumstances. Thank God Jesus hasn't changed, and that He will always be the same, to save, heal, deliver, and do anything we need Him to do. I love Angel, and thank God for her and wish her God's very best in her life.

Dodie Osteen
Co-Founder
Lakewood Church
Houston, Texas

Table of Contents

Testimony of Angela Marie Wood

I was born on November 20th, 1971, in Plainview, Texas to my parents: Rev. Gary and Deena Wood. My grand-parents, "PaPa" and "nanny" Kennedy, were there. I am told that everybody was happy that I was born.

I didn't develop properly as I should and tests that were run later at the University of Houston confirmed that at my birth I suffered mental retardation. The doctors would later tell my parents that I would never be able to go past a third grade level of learning. The test that I took said that I could not remember three things in a row. After starting school, teachers told my parents that I could never leave the classroom and go to the bathroom without getting lost. I was also told that I would never be able to read and memorize.

I had a coordination problem and I couldn't tie my shoes or throw or catch a ball. Besides the mental problems, I had several allergies that I had to take shots and medication for every day. Here's what the medical tests said: "Angel meets the criteria for a student with a handicap. Angel will not be able to go beyond some first grade subjects, and not beyond the third grade level in others." This report was given to my parents and, thank God they chose not to receive and believe it!

It was and is a bad report. I choose to believe God's word that says I can do all things through Christ which strengthens me. I believe nothing is impossible with God.

You know words that people speak about you or to you can hurt and tear you down. Our words must always build up and heal. Proverbs 6:2 says that you are snared by the words of your mouth...you are taken by the words of your mouth. According to Proverbs 8:8, all words of our mouth are to be righteous words. If you say, you can't have something then, you won't get it. You are a child of God, start acting like it. The Greater One lives in you. Decide to be all you can be for God. When you hide God's word in your heart, then you won't sin against God in word or deed.

I remember one time that I was crying because I wanted to ride a bicycle and be normal like the other kids my age. Dad came to my room and asked me what was wrong with me. I told him I wanted to be normal. He told me I was normal. Dad and mom called those things that were not as though they were.

I went outside to play with my friends. Up until that time I had never been able to ride a bike and I wanted to so bad. No one will ever know how much I hurt at times. That day, God healed me! One of my friends let me ride her bike. They said "Angel, you can do it." Thank God for my friends who encouraged me. Who you associate with will always have an influence upon you, either in a positive or negative way.

I started peddling and saying, "I can do all things through Christ which strengthens me." I didn't know how to stop the bike so I ran up a curb and hit a tree. When dad and mom came to me, I told them I was healed and could do all things through Christ. My dad told this story once in a message in Missouri and a couple who owned a bicycle shop gave me a new bike.

When you recognize you are a child of God and you can do all things through Christ which strengthens you, then you will not be defeated. Your problem can be turned into a blessing!

After my mom and dad received the bad report, they wrote on the papers that were given to them these words: "Angel is healed by the stripes of Jesus, according to I Peter 2:24 and Isaiah 53:5 & 6. We do not agree that Angel is mentally retarded, but that she is healed according to the word of God. Praise the Lord."

My parents did not deny the symptoms, but they denied them the right to rule over their daughter in their house. When you confess and stand on the words of God, it will make the devil mad. When the devil gets mad, you get glad. Remember! It's not the problem you are facing that will defeat you, but it's your attitude toward the problem that will determine the outcome.

While my mom and dad were pastoring, Full Gospel Fellowship in Stafford, Texas, my mom got an idea from God that was to help me receive my healing. She and Dad read scriptures on healing into a tape recorder and played them all night in my room. People everywhere began to pray for me. By this time I started memorizing scriptures like the doctors and teachers said I would never be able to do. I got up every morning and put on the full armor of God according to Ephesians 6. Doctors, teachers and psychologists had said that there were so many things in my life that I would never be able to accomplish. For me, to be able to read and write is a miracle.

God has healed my mind of mental retardation and healed me of allergies. I know God can save you, heal you and deliver you. You can have your miracle today! God healed me of my coordination problem and I can ride a bicycle. God has sure been good to me! And I know God isn't finished working with me yet, and He's not finished working with you. Don't give up! Keep on believing!

On May 18th, 1988, God called me into the ministry. I was in a revival with my dad when God spoke to me that I was to serve Him. Sometimes it seems like it takes longer to hear from God than we would like it to. Remember, God sent Jesus in the fullness of time and, there is a right time for you to come to maturity and a strong faith in God.

A college student once asked a college president, "Can I take a shorter course of studies than the one that's pre- scribed?" "Oh, yes," replied the president, "but it all depends on what you what to be." When God wants to make a giant oak tree, he takes many years. But when he wants to make a squash, He takes a few months. Who wants to be a squash? Remember that God wants you to be an oak tree, perfect and complete. That takes time. The Bible says believe you receive when you pray and the greatest expression of your faith is to thank God for what you believed you received, even though you cannot see it. When there is no evidence in the natural that what you are believing for will come to pass, you keep praising God. The Bible says in Psalm 50:23, "Whoso offereth praise glorifieth Me and to him that ordereth his conversation aright will I show My glory." This is the highest expression of your faith.

The Bible says, "Fight the good fight of faith." We are in a spiritual warfare. The devil will put you under pressure and do everything he can to keep you away from God. Why? Because he knows if you go to God your strength will be renewed. When you get strength you will be able to resist the devil and overcome. Make up your mind that you are going to stand, no matter how long it takes for it to manifest in the natural. Say, "Devil, if it's a fight you want, then it's a fight you will get...but I am standing on the word of God and when the dust settles, I will still be standing."

You have a choice in the dark times of your life to either believe God or the enemy and his lying symptoms. Maybe you know someone who tried and failed. Well, God never said to be triers of the Word. He said to be doers of the Word. You must stand and believe. The true child of God should be like tea. Your strength will come out when you get into hot water. The enemy wants to shake your confi- dence in God and tell you that God can't do what He said He would do for you in His Word. That's a trick of the devil. He will use your imagination against you. He'll have you plan your funeral. He will put pictures in your mind and will show and tell you there is so much you will never be able to do. God challenges us to call upon His name in prayer and He will show us great and might things that you know not. Jesus said that men ought always to pray and not faint. Anybody can give up. Anybody can say, "It's all over." Be careful not to use your mouth to talk "devil talk." Even though there may be a battle raging, we win.

Greater is He that is within us than he that is in the world.

Let me tell you confidently that God has a counter-attack for every attack the devil launches against you. Nothing surprises God. Nothing catches Him off guard. For every attack of the devil, God has one up on him.

The words that you speak are vehicles that bring into existence your miracle. They carry life or death, failure or success, sickness or health. Your eternal destiny can be changed by speaking right words. Also, your present circumstances can be changed by speaking right words. Jesus is the High Priest of our confession. When we speak God's word the Bible says angels work on our behalf to bring to pass what we are believing for. The trouble with some people is that they spend too much time saying what they don't have, instead of what they do have...and talking, about how bad things are instead of how good they are. It's like the story of the man who came home from work and he was tired. Nothing had gone right for him that day. His wife met him at the door and the children were screaming, he said to her, "Honey, if you can't say anything positive to me, just don't talk." She paused and said, "Alright, three of your four children didn't break their leg today." You may laugh, but the sad reality is that many times we negate our miracle by saying wrong words.

Say: "In the name of Jesus I renounce every negative word I have spoken or anyone else has spoken over me. I make a decision from this day forth to speak words of life and blessings. I refuse to speak words of doubt, fear and unbelief."

I believe the only hope for mankind is the return of Jesus Christ. I know He's coming soon. I don't know when it will happen, but it will happen. I'm waiting for that time, just like you. Until that day happens, I will continue to tell people what Jesus did for me, and pray to make the world a better place to live in by my example. I believe God has great things in store for us all in the days that are ahead.

Please pray with me: "Dear Lord Jesus, thank you for healing me. We believe that Your words will not return void but I believe they will do what You say they will. Father, I say with great boldness and confidence in Your word that by Your Stripes We Are Healed. Lord, I thank you that You came to destroy the works of the devil. We are the property of Almighty God, and I will give no place to the devil. I will stay in the secret place of the Most High God, where no power can harm me. In Jesus' name, Amen."

God Cares For You

Praise the Lord! I want to share with you in this book how God made me whole. I Peter 5:7 says: "Casting all your cares on Him for He cares for you." I want you to know that God cares about you. You are special to God. You are the apple of His eye. I know from my life that no matter what kind of trial you may go through, He cares for you.

Romans 15:13 says: "May the God of hope fill you with all joy and peace in believing, that you may abound in hope by the power of the Holy Spirit." You may be like I was at one time and feel like you're without hope. I am told hope is the most powerful word in the English lan- guage. It causes you to get up in the morning and go about your daily activities. It energizes you. Man can live forty days without food, four minutes without air, but only four seconds without hope. I was in a hopeless situation. It's when we can't do anything that God does everything. God can give you joy, peace and hope when all hope in the natural seems to be gone. No matter how long you have been in your present situation, God, your Heavenly Father, can bring you out victoriously. He can break the devil's strongholds in your life. You can be free from sickness or a defeated attitude that is trying to discourage you.

II Chronicles 25:9 says: "And the man of God answered, 'The Lord is able to give you much more than this.'" You know, many times we settle for second best in our lives. As a result our spirit is broken, we have shattered dreams and the problems seem overwhelming. Sometimes we feel like the crisis we are in is uncontrollable and the enemy we face seems unconquerable. I want you to know that God is in control of everything. Hebrews 13:6 says: "The Lord is our helper, and we will not fear."

God is able and willing to do much more for us than we are willing to let Him do. It's time for you to change your thinking and make a bold decision to push on through. Stop bowing down to the problem and do what God has commanded you to do. We must exercise our faith. Faith is a struggle. It's not trying to convince yourself that you're healed by reciting numerous times, "I'm healed." Faith is believing God and taking Him at His word. It's time for you to obey God's word and receive all that's available for you. As for me I will not back up, give up or shut up. It's time to press on toward the finish line. There is no one else on the face of the earth that can do what God has called you to do in His Kingdom. I refuse to be defeated or discouraged. I'm going to put my faith and trust in Jesus. I'm expecting Him to do exactly what He said He would do.

Maybe you're facing a discouraging situation, or going through a storm or trial right now. You may have spiritual bruises from struggles you're going through. There are times when we just don't understand what's happening in our lives. Have you ever gone through a time in your life that you've searched for God and wondered, "Lord, where are you?" At those times we want to just stay in bed, pull the covers over our head and resign from the human race. But it takes real courage to keep on standing and doing the right thing when everything around you seems to not be going right. It's at those times you must lean on Jesus and believe God's word over your circumstances. I have decided to walk by faith and trust God's word.

God is not in turmoil over your problem. He is not asleep. He is not sitting on His throne in heaven, wringing His hands and saying, "Oh Jesus, what are We going to do?" He who turned water into wine, fed thousands with a small lad's lunch, provided manna from heaven and water from a gushing rock, put coins in a fish's mouth, opened blind eyes, unstopped deaf ears and raised the dead...is ready to meet your need. Begin to praise God because where the spirit of praise is, He will show up.

Nothing happens by coincidence or luck in the life of a believer. God, according to Jeremiah 29:11, has a plan for your life. When you go through a difficult time in your life, it will either cause you to turn away from God or to focus your attention on Him. God is more interested in developing our character than He is in our comfort. God wants us to grow to spiritual maturity where He can use us for His Glory. He wants His love to shine through us. I have decided to let Him do that in my life.

PRAY THIS: I WILL NOT ALLOW THE ENEMY TO HAVE A FOOTHOLD IN MY LIFE. THE DEVIL HAS NO POWER OVER ME. GREATER IS HE THAT IS IN ME THAN HE THAT IS IN THE WORLD. GOD HAS A SPECIAL PLAN FOR MY LIFE. I WILL FULFILL THAT PLAN IN JESUS' NAME.

Boldness

I want to share with you about walking in boldness. The Bible says in Proverbs 28:1, "The wicked flee when no one pursues but the righteous are bold as a lion."

The Bible says, "Faith cometh by hearing and hearing by the word of God" (Romans 10:17). You don't have to pray to get faith. Faith comes by studying and hearing the word of God and the more we hear God's word the more our faith increases. You don't try to have faith in God. The Bible says, "Have faith in God." You try to like vegetables. But you have faith in God and then you must act on your faith. Jesus said to one man: 'Rise up, take your bed and walk," and he did. He could have sat there and said, "The day of miracles has passed away." There never was a day of miracles; there is a God of miracles. He could have said, "I've never walked before because some- one always gets ahead of me and beats me out of receiving my miracle." Instead he got up and walked. He received his miracle.

If you say it won't happen to you then it won't happen to you...but if in faith you believe what God's word says is true and you say it's for me today then you can receive it because God has promised it.

When my dad was in heaven he saw a room with a sign on the door that said "Unclaimed Blessings." He saw angels going in to get the specific miracles people needed on the earth...and then just as it was being delivered to them, they rejected it by saying, "It's not for me, the day of miracles has passed."

If you need faith in a certain area, you need to read God's word on that subject and it will build faith in your spirit man to receive. The more we hear God's word, the more our faith increases. Faith in God means a great deal to the Wood family. Without faith in God's word on healing, my dad would have died from a heart attack in 1977 and cancer in 1998. God gloriously healed him and he's walking in divine health. Without faith in God's word my PaPa, Ken Kennedy, would have died in 1998 from an aneurysm. God healed him. God gave PaPa a creative miracle. He was born with one kidney but tests recently have revealed that God created a new one in his body. Hallelujah! Without faith in God's word, my friend Dodie Osteen of Lakewood Church in Houston would have died of cancer. She is healed and serves the Lord faithfully. Without faith in God's word, my brother David would be an alcoholic or even dead...but praise God, we stood on the word of God in Isaiah 54:13. David graduated from Texas Bible Institute in Columbus, Texas, and from Lee University in Cleveland, Tennessee.

Without faith in God's word that renewed my mind, I would be in an institution for the mentally retarded. But with God all things are possible.

It's only through faith that you can take the struggles and hits that come your way and hang on until you make it. And I want you to know that you can make it. Press on toward the finish line. Press on toward the mark for the prize of the high calling of God in Christ Jesus (Philippians 3:14). Right now, why don't you just stop reading and lift your hands, rejoice and magnify the name of Jesus for it's in His Mighty, Matchless Name that we win.

With faith in God's word you can stand up to the devil and not faint. You can say to Satan, "In the name of Jesus, I resist you. You must flee. Devil, you're not in charge over my life. I'm in authority over you through the power of Jesus."

I've walked through some deep valleys and dark places in my life and I didn't always know what to do but I've learned to trust God's word and do what it says and God has always been good to me. As my friend Pastor John Osteen used to say, "I am what the Bible says I am. I can have what the Bible says I can have." Everything that pertains to life and godliness is in the Bible and it's available to you and me. When you read the Bible, you will be changed. God's word will set you free.

Sometimes I still get knocked down but it's only temporary. The enemy tries to wound my spirit by words that are spo- ken to me or by telling me I'm not normal but I have a tremendous spirit of victory in my soul. I have been washed in the blood of Jesus, my mind is renewed, and I am victorious through the mighty name of Jesus.

I've endured hardship and it has made me stronger. God has been preparing me, growing me up and making the woman out of me He wants me to be. He has prepared me and anointed me for this day and time that I'm living in. God said to me, "I'm stretching your faith muscles to make you strong in Me."

I want more boldness in my life. You can pray for boldness and operate in it. One day I was with my mom and dad after church at a restaurant in Houston, Texas and while we were standing in line waiting to get our food, suddenly, a lady at the front of the line had a seizure. She fell on the floor and began to bite her tongue. I felt the boldness of God rise up in me and I bolted out of line, shocking my parents by running towards her. I put my hand on her and said "Attention, Hell!" I learned that from my dear friends Pastor Ed and Brenda Adamson, who pastor Paris Christian Center in

Paris, Tennessee. I call them aunt and uncle because they are family to me.

I not only got the attention of the demons attacking that lady, but all the people who had gotten there earlier and were either standing in line or sitting at their tables. There were people in that line that I am sure went to churches that didn't believe in or understand what I was doing. Everybody moved out of my way. God touched the lady, as I obeyed the word, laid hands on her and cast out the demons that were tormenting her. She stood up, wiped away her tears, thanked me and got up normal. Everybody moved back and let me and my family come up to the front of the line.

I believe God wants to put a new anointing of boldness upon every one of you so that you will begin to see things that you have never seen in the spirit and do the greater works of God according to John 14:12.

Our job and mission on this earth is to unload hell and load up heaven. We are to be dispensers of God's Good News to all we meet. Jesus came to this earth to save His people from their sins (Matthew 1:21). God's desire is for all people to be saved. He is not willing that any should perish, but that all should come to repentance (II Peter 3:9). There is only one way of salvation and it is to receive what Jesus did on the cross by shedding His blood for the remission of your sins.

I remember when I first met Brenda Adamson. She was selling real estate. She sold my dad a church. My dad told me about her and when I met her I asked if she was saved and Spirit-filled. She said she was. I said, "Okay, speak in tongues, I want to hear you." We prayed together right there and God knitted our hearts together. I'm talking about boldness.

I believe it is possible to walk in such boldness that a doubting, skeptical world can see God's glory on us and it will cause them to take notice that we are the people of God. I have decided to walk in this kind of boldness. How about you?

One night I was ministering with my dad in a motel room we rented to conduct a healing service. After I sang I stepped outside to get a drink of water. Next to the room where we were meeting, there was a bar. A drunken man stepped from the bar and came over to me and said some ugly and vulgar remarks. The boldness of the Holy Ghost rose up in me and I said, "Sir, you have a dirty, black heart that needs to be washed in the precious red blood of Jesus and it will make you white as snow."

I then took him by the hand and led him into the room where my dad was preaching. I told him what the man did. My dad told me later that he really wanted to lay hands on him in the form of a fist. Hey...he's still just a man. I love you, Dad. Instead, dad prayed for him and the man was set free.

Later that same night when I was in the bathroom, I met a lady who was smoking. I told her that if God wanted her nose to be a chimney, He would have built it out of bricks and put it on the top of her head. I then asked her to come with me and she did. I introduced her to my dad by saying, "Dad, this one smells like she's been to hell." We prayed for her and God set her free.

I had to make a decision to walk in boldness and do what God has commanded me to do and so will you. I decided I wasn't going to lie around and feel sorry for myself. It would have been easy for me to do that because when I was born, doctors and psychologists said I was mentally retarded. They said there were so many things I would never be able to learn or do. I have surprised them because I made a decision to not be limited by my circumstances and let them rule my life.

I challenge you to rise up above your circumstances. It doesn't matter what the doctors, lawyers or bankers say. They may say "it's incurable" or "you can't have the loan." Your dreams may have been shattered over things that have happened in the past and you are wallowing in that problem. Stop lying down in the ashes of fear, sickness and doubt. Make a decision to change your attitude, thinking and believing. It's time to quit carrying that problem as a security blanket wrapped over your shoulder and start carrying it, instead of it carrying you.

Sometimes in our lives we all face problems that appear to be unsolvable. Remember that it's not the problem you're facing that will defeat you, but it's your attitude towards it that will determine the outcome.

You can choose to be a success. You can choose to walk in victory instead of failure. You can choose to be obedient. You don't have to fail in life and be discouraged and defeated. You can have good health and peace of mind. You can choose to be a winner and not a loser. You can have joy and not sadness. You can do all things through Christ who strengthens you. Praise the Lord!

My brother David once said something that means a lot to me. He said: "If you want to be a winner, then dream big and then follow through until you conquer and overcome any hindrances."

You must plant in your spirit what you want to see reproduced in your life. You have the ability to make right or wrong choices. It's your decision. I choose to receive the blessings of God and not the curses of the enemy. I choose health and not sickness. I choose soundness of mind and not confusion.

Boldness

Proverbs 4:14-15 says: Enter not into the path of the wicked, And go not in the way of evil men. Avoid it, pass not by it, turn From it and pass by.

Who wants to go the way of evil men? Not me! Evil men walk in darkness and not light. They don't know what they are doing because they are not operating with the mind of Christ. We are the light of the world, so let's let our light shine so that all men will glorify God through the good works we do. I'm going to let my light shine. Are You?

I want to share with you seven steps to help you be all that God wants you to be.

1) Set your mind on the goal you want to accomplish!

You don't have to stay in the condition you are in. You don't have to live in sickness and poverty. You can change the circumstances in your life by finding a promise from God's word and making a decision to stand on it. There are over 3,000 promises in the word of God and every one of them belongs to those who believe. If you need a healing, find healing scriptures. If you need prosperity, find scriptures on prosperity. Read them out loud and claim them as yours. It's good to read them into a tape recorder and play them back again. They will get down into your spirit and bring your manifestation. I like to confess I have the mind of Christ.

2) You must press on in hot pursuit to accomplish your goal.

The Bible says in Matthew 11:12, "The Kingdom of God is taken by violence and the violent take it by force." Make the decision that you're not going to be average. Average is the best of the worst and the worst of the best.

Don't be passive. Determine you'll not settle for second best. Quit saying, "One of these days, I'll do this or that." Make a decision that you'll start obeying God today. This is the day that the Lord has made. Rejoice and be glad in it. Keep on going until your dream is fulfilled. Start by believing God for small things, then your faith will increase to believe for larger things.

3) Watch whom you associate with and be careful what you see and hear.

The Bible says in Proverbs 13:20, "He who walks with wise men will be wise, but the companion of fools will be destroyed." Some people will drain your faith. They have no goals, dreams or ambitions and all they want is for you to be like them. I can't be around those kinds of people because they get me off course and the plan God has for my life. If the people you're running around with won't change, get away from them because they will drain your faith and make you as weak as they are. There is nothing wrong with taking advice from people as long as it agrees with the word of God, but if it doesn't, then don't listen to them. Some people want to give you a piece of their mind, but most of us can't afford to give any of it away. Art Linkletter laughed at a man who had an idea to build a family theme park. He told him it would never work. The dreamer was a man named Walt Disney, who created Disneyland and Disneyworld. I've been there. It's real, and a whole lot of fun. Don't you know that Art Linkletter wishes that he had become Walt Disney's partner? Recently, I met Bill and Gloria Gaither at their home in Alexandria, Indiana. Bill had an idea about getting all the old-time Gospel singers together and recording them. People told him no one would buy the videos and then sit down and watch them. These singers are blessing mil- lions of people, because Bill pursued his dream.

4) Forget the past.

The worst thing you can do is to worry about past mistakes. The Apostle

Paul said, "Forget those things which are behind and reach to those things which are ahead" (Philippians 3:13).

In 1990 at the college World Series, an outstanding third baseman that had the lowest percentage of all third basemen in the nation made three errors in a row. They finally had to pull him out of the game because he got his mind on his mistakes and he kept making the same errors over and over again. When the devil reminds you of your past and paints a picture of all your mistakes, remind him of his future. Tell him you've been washed in the blood and your sins are as far away from you as the east is from the west. Forget the past.

5) Lay aside every weight or hindrance that keeps you from being a success, healed, having peace of mind, and walking in victory!

You know, sometimes my room and closet gets cluttered up with things and I have to clean them out. God told me to unclutter my life. Our hearts get cluttered with bitterness and other garbage so we must get rid of it or it will defeat us. Psalms 66:18 says, "If I regard iniquity in my heart, the Lord will not hear me." People's words and actions toward me have hurt me but I have decided not to hold on to that garbage because it will only destroy my soul. I choose to let it go and pray for those who hurt me. I know it isn't easy, but it's the right thing to do. God wants our hearts clean and pure so we will be free to run the race He has called us to run.

6) You need to be aglow and burning with the Holy Spirit in your life.

Ephesians 5:18 says, "Be not drunk with wine wherein is excess but be filled with the spirit." Being filled with the spirit is not an option: it's a command.

7) We must be in the right position where God wants us to be.

The Bible tells us in Hebrews that we are not to forsake the assembling of ourselves together as some but exhort one another so much the more as you see the day approaching. Jesus is coming again to take us that believe in Him to live with Him forever and I want to be living a pure, holy life when He returns. I want to sing for Him, dance before Him, clap my hands for Him, and love Him here on earth until I see Him face to face.

II Corinthians 2:14 says: God always causes us to triumph in Christ. Triumph means to try again. Maybe you have failed in one area. But try again until you find the place you are sup- posed to be in. If it's singing in the choir, ushering, being a deacon, a missionary, or one of the five-fold ministries, be faithful where God has placed you.

Next time the devil tries to put condemnation, sickness or confusion on you, say "No thanks, Mr. Devil, I choose to triumph in Christ Jesus. If the devil knocks you down, get up, dust yourself off and try again. The Holy Spirit lives in you and you cannot be defeated.

Confess this out loud:
 I will not give up.
 I make a choice to follow Jesus.
 I have stepped over the line.
 I won't let up, back up, give up or shut up.
 My focus is clear and heaven is my goal.
 My path is straight and my joy is complete.

I am a follower and a disciple of Christ.

I'm sure you have situations in your life that you are going through and you can't make it without God's help. I want to pray for you. I know prayer works. It has worked in my life and continues to do so.

Let's pray:

Father, I come to you in Jesus' name. I pray that you will meet every need of everyone who is reading this book. Jesus, I thank you for the perfect plan you have for our lives. Lord we yield ourselves to you and ask that you will reveal your goals and plans for each of us and let us deter- mine to walk in them.

I take authority over every demon spirit that is attacking those who read this book. I declare that no weapon formed against us shall prosper. Satan, I proclaim because of what Jesus accomplished at the cross that we will walk in victory. We command you in Jesus name to back up and cease your attack against us. We plead the blood of Jesus. We stand on the word of God and we will not give up. I come against every stronghold that has exalted itself against the knowledge of God. I choose to trust you Lord with my whole heart. I receive the mind of Christ. I reject the word of the doctors, lawyers and psychologists if it's against the word of God. I declare that I am whole and sound of mind. I claim the word of God to minister healing to my whole body. I claim by Jesus' stripes that we are healed.

I receive the blessings of Christ. All ground that the enemy has taken we take it back in Jesus' name. I confess that my body is the temple of the Hold Spirit...redeemed, cleansed, and forgiven by the blood of Jesus. Therefore, Satan has no more place in me, no power over, and no assignment against me will prosper.

I claim all my needs met in Jesus' name. The most important decision you can ever make is to receive Jesus Christ as your Lord. He will never turn any- one away. "For whosoever shall call upon the name of the Lord shall be saved (Romans 10:13)."

Pray this prayer now:

Dear God,

I want to become a born again Christian. I come to you in the name of Jesus Your Son. I confess I am a sinner. I believe you sent Your Son to die on the cross for my sins. I confess with my mouth and believe in my heart that Jesus Christ is Lord. In Jesus name I pray. Amen.

I encourage you to join a Bible-believing Church and be water-baptized as an expression of your trust in Jesus.

Enjoy an Exciting Life in Christ!

Testimonies

I loved your daughter and her simple prayers for miracles when she appeared on prime time television. You know God really speaks through her.

God bless her!

    Dorothy Salje

        Odessa, Texas

Dear Gary,

My wife and I met you at Roswell, New Mexico several years ago. Your daughter was 16. She prayed for my elbow and God healed it right then. I also remembered how good you sang. May God spiritually and financially bless you as you go about His business.

Your fellow saint in Christ,

    Wayne & Betty Eakin

        Roswell, New Mexico

Angel's dad, Reverend Gary Wood writes:

I was ministering with Brother Charles Reed on KMCI TV, Monroe, Louisiana. We were sharing the salvation prayer at the close of the Fully Alive Program. All the phone counselors had left the phones as the credits were running on the TV screen. The counselors were joining together to pray over the needs that had been called in during the program. The phone rang and our daughter, Angel, answered the phone and the lady she prayed with accepted the Lord as her personal Savior and then received the baptism in the Holy Spirit with the evidence of speaking in tongues.

Angel's ministry to this woman is a miracle in itself because of how God has marvelously healed her mind and body as you can see when you read her testimony. She truly loves the Lord.

The next day Barbara Pritchard the main counselor told us what happened. She called the lady, who lives in Bastrop, LA, to verify the information such as: correct name, address, etc. To her amazement the lady told her that she had cut both her wrists and blood was dripping from her wrists at the time she called the previous night. She felt an urge to turn the TV on. When she did she saw us leading in the salvation prayer. She called the number on the screen. As she prayed with

Angel for salvation, the blood stopped dripping completely from her wrist. God is a merciful and miracle working God! Praise His Holy Name!

About the Author

Angel Wood is a living, walking miracle from God. What the devil said she could not do, God has said she can. In fact, she has her own business that God is really blessing. Through Angel's life, you can have encouragement to receive a miracle, too. Angel lives in Sugar Land, Texas with her parents, Rev. Gary and Deena Wood, PO BOX 1649, Sugarland, TX 77487.

www.garywoodministries.com